BATH OF HERBS

ALSO BY EMILY ZOBEL MARSHALL

EMILY ZOBEL MARSHALL

BATH OF HERBS

PEEPAL TREE

First published in Great Britain in 2023
Peepal Tree Press Ltd
17 King's Avenue
Leeds LS6 1QS
UK

ISBN: 9781845235574

Printed in the United Kingdom
by Severn, Gloucester,
on responsibly sourced paper

Supported by
ARTS COUNCIL
ENGLAND

CONTENTS

I. MOTHER SUN

To mother, Jenny Zobel

BATH OF HERBS

To my grandmother Enny, who gave my mother
a bath of herbs to help her heal after my birth.

Grandmother, healer, I give thanks,
for while I mewed newborn in my basket,
she lay birth-ruptured,
so you prepared a bath of herbs
gathered in your garden
under beating summer skies.

With mortar and pestle you crushed
calming yellow chamomile into young mint,
pressed buds of newly flowered lavender,
sprinkled ocean salt with rubbing fingers,
mixed Caribbean cloves in oil of orange,
made back then for now.

Gently you mix, scrape, paste,
add plant to water, spoon, test, swirl
until bath and steam are essence bursting
and all is ready.

And so you lead her,
coiled and naked, hurting, tender,
slowly sink her into hot, forgetting waters,
unfurl her long aching body
enveloped in steam. Your love hits her lungs,
into every crevice of her form diffuses,
skin and soul now blessed, baptised.
Mother, released, renewed,
she will step out strong again
to greet the world and me
as I sleep deeply in my basket

Grandmother, daughter-healer,
I give thanks.

DON'T LET THE BOY CUT THE CANE

A poem for Maman Tine, my great great grandmother,
who refused to let my grandfather, Joseph Zobel, cut cane in the cane fields.

I.
Don't let the boy cut cane;
let him stand in a white uniform
starched overnight in zinc buckets.
Don't let his hands be split by the cutlass,
and furrow and crack
like dark cane field earth,
baked by beating suns.
Let his fingers be oiled and smell sweet
but not of sugar,
not burnt in the boiling house.
Let them poise pen over paper,
wear fine gloves in white French winters,
sharpen red pencils, swing strong leather satchels,
while I force my slow, rolling hips into the fields,
for the cane must be cut.

II.

You let us take root, Maman Tine,
in the wreckage of your body,
to reach up towards the light.

Maman Tine's hands were black, swollen, hardened,
cracked at every joint
and every crack encrusted with a sort of
indelible mud. [1]

Let us read the pages of your story
as we trace your wounds
in the lines of our palms,

her scratched hands, every day clinging
to the handle of the hoe,
an easy prey to the fierce cuts inflicted
by the cane leaves.

Let me hear the slash of your cutlass, Maman Tine,
as I tend to my Yorkshire dahlias
wearing pink gardening gloves.

See her hands, as if thrown there
with sacrilegious carelessness
on the whiteness of that sheet
in the depth
of that obscure shack.

The italicised passages in this poem are excerpted and adapted from
Joseph Zobel's *Black Shack Alley* (1950; 2020)

UNDOCUMENTED
for Mami Enny

The tiny drawer inside your dresser is secret
but it pops open on the lightest touch.
Inside, we discover the bundle of his letters,
snug in their velveteen pouch.
We hurriedly unfold, read,
wary of the burden of confidences.

Each scrawl speaks of his longing
for you — his wife, and the island left behind —
carried over oceans by a tide of hope
to the cold white metropole.

And so we read:
You, you are more beautiful than brash Parisian women;
they are wealthy, but lack your humble grace,
and if the grand boulevards take my breath away,
when I lie, alone, in my narrow bed,
it's the softness of your hand, the light of fireflies,
the steady flight of the mansfenil
that fill my mind.

One month later it's: *Let's get a little trade going,*
send me cinnamon, a packet of vanilla pods —
in Paris they'll fetch triple.
In return, parcels of kitchen things, a radio —
you'll be the envy of our neighbours.
Invite Monsieur Armand to wire and tune
and Madame Christophe to covet.
Place it (carefully!) on the second dresser shelf
and when she's gone (only when she's gone),
find a station with biguine and dance with both our boys,
and I, in my icy room, will imagine the sway
and tilt of your hips in the warmth of our kitchen.

Instructions on thinning pages
kept for decades, but nothing about your life,
of two wild boys and baby Jenny heavy in your stomach,
the unremitting heat, long sweaty, lonely nights,
the eldest rubbing your swollen feet
and money worries, always money worries.

He will call for you and you will pack
off to the world's centre,
stand beside the writer on his grand journey.
You'll bake cakes, raise children and play host,
sing Creole lullabies, tell island stories
(simple tales, he says, but you are not quite so sure).
No long letters reveal your secrets, Mami.
Did he not treasure your replies?
And so the life I long to read still hides,
undocumented. There are no maps;
a granddaughter can only dream
into the gaps.

MAMI'S WARNING

Listen, *ma dou-dou,*
don't open the fridge
without your cardigan.
Haven't you heard about
your Great Aunt Mary-Lou from Guadeloupe,
who opened the fridge,
caught a chill and nearly died
right *there* in her kitchen?

Girl, don't fiddle with the car door.
Fide, your second cousin from Dakar,
three-years-old, sitting on his mother's lap
in the back seat, messed with the door.
They both fell out,
rolled like coconuts into the gully.
Still has trouble walking,
gravel marks across his face.
Poor Fide.

You think you can eat
before your swim, *ma cherie?*
You want to die, *is that it?*
Neighbour Madi-Nina had three boys –
not the two you play with.
Number 3, Petit Paul, ate before swimming.
Hot afternoon,
stuffed his face with fritters,
jumped in the pool,
killed, *blam*, by the shock.
Body must rest after food
Go for your siesta!

You think I'm crazy
with my wasp swatting?

Laughing at me trying
to kill each one?
You can laugh and end up like Uncle Milo,
stung by a wasp and swelled *twice* his size.
Now he stays indoors, *safe*
from winged murderers.

Ha! I see you climbing up
to fetch the glass jar,
to help yourself to my dried bananas.
So you never saw my little sister, Julie?
Climbed up, jar smashed on her head.
Big-big scar from eye to ear.
It's why she never married.
And, *dou-dou*, never say, *dit jamais*,
that your Mami didn't warn you.

BROWN TIGHTS

The doll I loved,
took her everywhere
in my pram,
named her *poupée* Jenny
after you, Mum.
She even wore bloomers
under her billowing madras skirt
and a Kente headscarf.
Poupée Jenny drank tea
from a tiny tea set,
sitting inside the hollows of oak trees.
Sometimes I pulled her
in a cardboard box carriage
to the dolls' ball.

Years later,
Poupée Jenny sits
in my pizza-box-strewn
spliff-stale student room;
I see her face pealing;
I pull back layers
of brown tights,
delicately darned lips,
eyes stripped away;
beneath them a gollywog,
white-eyed, grinning
blackface vaudeville.

I find a needle, thread,
stitch the homemade face
back in place
double-quick.

PICNIC

I don't want to wear my summer dress
but you say, "Today, we dress bright",
and with your Afro swept back
in a fiery patterned scarf
march me to the *rhaeadr*, the waterfall.

There's no proper picnic mat,
only a soggy-when-you-kneel
moth-balled throw,
no jam and peanut butter sandwiches
but chunks of raw carrot shoved in the marg tub.

But when you unwrap
leftover Easter egg surprise,
I see, before you turn away,
a fat tear rolling down your nose.

You strip, wade long and brown
into icy waters,
trout lacing around at your ankles.

Back on the bank you stretch out winter legs,
unfurling fern fronds,
drop crumbs of Easter egg
into your mouth.

You squint at the pale sun
your Afro jewelled with droplets.
You sing *à la claire fontaine*.

I stay busy with my net
catching nine tadpoles
and a plump, shiny yellow frog.

Quickly, I let her go,
for she must glide away
and hide no strange and silent tears
from her spawn.

MAMWLAD

We hunt for pieces of broken china
scattered amongst the stones
of *Afon Croesor*, icy with summit snow-melt
under a bruised and sunless April sky.

You find thick pieces of plate, blue and white,
swirling with the wings of courting birds.
You sit on the riverbank trying to fit resisting
shards back together in your open palms.

You tell me you love this once colonised land
which, like yours, holds fast to its tongue
like lichen on stone walls.

Squint, you say, and see how these fronds of river fern
could unfurl against skies of cobalt Caribbean blue.
At night, you could hear cicadas chant
in chorus with the bleat of sleepy mountain sheep.

I know you still feel the pull of it, Maman,
of your island, *l'île aux fleurs*, yet here you are
on a cold riverbank, wrapped up warm and
wading in green wellies.

You are knotted to this valley, this *cwm,* flanked
by mountains with bellies burst open, their quarried
entrails scattered all the way to the grey sea.
You are tied by bonds of kinship, by sugar,
blood, survival and slate.

So when you stand in the flow of
Afon Croesor, holding china fragments tight,
you are not home, but know the river sings
with all the echoes of *mamwlad.*

THE HEALING

In the corner of her hospital room
you sit like a prayer, half-moon reading glasses
on the end of your nose, novel in hand,
steady against all proclamations
on your five-year-old granddaughter's fate.

You drape cheap, market-bought
Kente throws over white metal bedframes,
place bunches of bluebells in paper cups,
which Doc will immediately discard:
a contamination risk.

You burn incense, produce tubs
of garlic-laden lentil soup, her favourite,
as doctors hang chemotherapy charts,
plug machines, plunge needles,
discuss the myriad *side effects.*

When we bring her home,
long hair falling out in clumps
thick enough to plug the bath,
you bring your quiet smile,
your lavender *huile de massage,*
your strong brown hands
and pummel the toxins out of her,
stretching her thin white,
blue-veined body,
rolling your fists,
smoothing your palms
over moonish skin,
pushing your healing through fingertips
deep into her
treacherous blood.

MOTHER SUN

The machine bleeps
and, right on cue,

Nice Nurse fills
the fat syringe

with just enough morphine
to return you

to Dakar sun
and your teenage years,

you, drawing the
gaze of men,

asteroids magnetised
by your aura.

This vision of enflamed hearts
makes you chuckle.

*You can love many different men
in different ways*, you said.

Flushed, I gulped my canteen coffee,
heard the stillness

in between the bleeps
in between the endless stream

of bedside visitors – planets
orbiting for warmth

around you, the star in
Kente headscarf set against

yellowed chemoed skin,
propped up on the bright pillow.

You know, one lady visitor, you say
who has (your voice dips to a whisper)

fallen deeply in love with you.
For even now, while losing hair

and almost weightless,
even now, as death moves in,

you're certain
of your pull.

TRAVEL PREPARATIONS

We prepare
by singing Bob Marley
in thin voices
because every little thing
is going to be alright.
I arrange bouquets of flowers,
dab your hot lobes
with *eau de cologne,*
work lavender oil into
cracked soles,
smooth your dry hair
(nurse changes bedsheets)
and together we tug
a white silk nightdress
onto your disappearing body
because you never
enjoyed travelling
unprepared.

A SWEET MANGO FOR MAMI

For my mother Jenny (1947 - 2019)

In hospice final days
you longed to eat
the mango I brought you,
feel sweet juice
trickle down your parched throat,
journeying you home
to Martinican shores.

No! said Doc Katrina.
Far too fibrous for a sick
and ailing woman who hasn't eaten for days.
So I took it home to eat for you
but could only watch
sunlight-yellow skin
wrinkle and brown,
sweet juices burst through flesh
and sticky-up the fruit bowl.

Mami's rotted mango
was finally committed
to the compost heap,
to let pink worms eat it,
and fat black ants
become crazed and drunk
on its far-away sugars.

Autumn comes
and I rake compost into
dark Northern earth,
enriched by a mango meant for Mami.
It's reaching for roots ready
to push strong stems
into the light of Spring.

MOURNING

On the first day of your passing
I wept among the graves,
kneeling in long grasses.

On the second day,
I searched your handbag
and found small solace
in neatly folded photographs,
stuffed in pockets of your leather purse,
and scent of *eau de cologne.*

On the third,
I looked for your eyes
in the faces of my children.

On the fourth,
I laughed at one of your
daft, half-remembered jokes.

On the fifth,
I flew to Greece
and saw you in lights
reflected by the ocean.

On the sixth,
I caught your voice
on the breeze.

But only on the seventh
did I feel you beside me,
your warm breath
meshed with mine.

VICAR'S LETTERS NOS. 1 & 2

Plant a Mediterranean garden
on my grave, said Mum
with her remaining rasping breath;
mint, lavender, thyme, rosemary,
tarragon, marjoram and sage;
let their roots release me, scent
me into Yorkshire breezes.

We go wild with planting
for the only Martinican woman
in the graveyard of St Chads.
Herbs sturdy with her compost
shoot towards June sunlight.

Vicar's letter no.1 arrives
in an August heatwave.
*We must ensure that all plants
on all graves are no taller than 30cm.*

A dance of autumn leaves delivers
Vicar's letter no. 2.

*Failure to comply/unsightly plants/taller than regulation
not the bedding variety/have been duly removed
along with the following mementos:*
1. *A hama bead rainbow*
(left by a grieving granddaughter)
2. *A wooden spinning ladybird*
(the sort of tat she loved)
3. *An earthenware diffuser*
(turned by her beloved brother)

[Please note that the church does allow the planting of Spring bulbs]

Fingers of April sunshine
reach between graves
setting ablaze Mum's
Spring-bulbed carnival of flowers,
claiming this corner of English earth
and releasing her, scented,
into Yorkshire breezes.

MENDING THE ARK

I have let this ark sink and little has been spared.
From the garage I drag damp books, letters, photos, find
creeping seas of mildew spread through clinging pages.

Delicate clusters of mould bloom in the dark, billowing from
the swelling sides of boxes, spewing fretful spores as the rain
drips steady through the leaking roof over the archive of your life.

I salvage frantically. Back home, I unfold our history on my bed,
let it dry out. Two pictures pull me: one small, faded, black and white.
Mami breastfeeding you, on a wicker chair, in her yard in Martinique.

She holds your tiny plump hand. Behind her a contented chicken pecks.
She is at ease with this photographer and awash with pride.
You have released her nipple as your face beams up at her.

Then one of you, 70s sepia, with a carefully sculpted afro, your
white-surprise baby at your breast. A carefully knotted handkerchief
covers the delicate dome of my head. Your eyes half-closed, suspended
between ecstasy and new-Mum exhaustion. Smiling into sunlight,
as if life will only offer more of this.

Noah saved pairs and so have I. Two mothers, two babies,
a chain of nourishment. Grandmother and mother reach towards me.
They tell me I can mend the ark.

ON LEAVING ON THE CUSP OF SPRING

On the crag I find the stillness that I crave
in the curves of ice-hewn ridges
that drew these boulders to a halt
on a rise of undulating hills;

in the tremor of the kestrel's wing
who bargained with the wind
to stay rooted in a patch of blue;

in the clenched fist of early morning mist
opening its fingers, rising from the fans of trees,
bursting with the dreams of budding leaves;

in the new-born lamb who seeks his mother's milk
with painful pulls and jerks until it flows
and ewe and lamb can breathe as one;

and in knowing that although you did not see
this miracle of early Spring but left us on its cusp,
I can be your eyes, your heart,
and all of this belongs to both of us.

FOX

You left me in the Spring,
last breath on hospice bed,
crisp sheets tight and fanned by morning light.

Now I run on winter nights
no focus for my love.
Red trainers beat on frosty streets,
remembering the rhythms of your heart,
adrift inside my pain.

My shadow crosses pavements
into a stretch of urban moonlit park
and there's a fox
who stops to stare,
locking yellowed eyes with mine,
bristling with fiery otherness
and stinking proud,

and I am stilled, can breathe at last,
but it's not you that sent him
for he turns and streaks
across the muddied grass.

II. MOON-PULLED

ANANSI MOTHERS

Lost in evening woods,
crushed, strength has left me;
in dying autumn light I see,
stretched from wire to wooden post,
Anansi's web, jewelled with rain,
light bouncing to the touch, filigree.

Umbilical spider thread,
trace me back to fields of cane,
weave the tale that binds me
to cross-stitched stories fine as lace;
to Jenny, Enny, M'man Tine,
spinning homes in hostile places,
minds strong, hands busy
and backs held arrow straight.

When I am bowed by my vexations,
Anansi mothers, pull me up,
whisper stories of our power
and with your silver rope now raise me,
home me amongst jewels of rain,
unbend my back
then set me free
and I will find my path again.

YOUR MAMA IS A BIG WAVE SURFER

I won't go in
because I can't stand to wait,
so I ride it out solo
until I heave on the stairs,
do twisting dog on the hall carpet,
scream primal screams in our car,
body contorting up-up-up and seatbelt straining,
and you yelling
Why did you leave it so late?
We should have gone in earlier;
this bloody baby
is coming.

Too dilated to wait in the room,
too advanced to walk to the pool –
pool not full yet so let me stand.
Don't touch me,
I am balanced and
I can begin.

The waves are 20 feet high.
I grip my board,
ready for the upsurge
to scoop me, try to
throw me, engulf me,
but look, here I come
back out of the barrelling surf,
a champion of the sport.
You might as well
get your camera and capture this,
because
this is
epic.

The moments of in-between are
calm. I am a floating body,
light on the salty ocean,
set for the next wall
of water to strike my core.

Tsunami conquered,
in a tearing wave of blood and sweat,
you arrive.

Pleased to meet you,
my beauty.
I'm your mama;
big wave
surfer.

HALF-MOON MONTHS

I watched my half-moon rise out of bathwater,
felt the heart-beat, womb-kick of you,
the weighty welcome stretch of you.

You came quick with golden curls,
you carry my face,
your rolling slope of forehead
whispers Africa, your lip-arch
deep-struck by love's bow.

Your latch is weak and undrunk milk
builds hard in the calabash of my breasts,
until you learn to suckle fast and grow.

Yet I still yearn for half-moon months,
the slow rise of stomach-hill, the skin-tight curve.
The miracle and pull of you,
that two heartbeat drum,
how I miss the pulse of you.

WHEN MY BOY WAS SHORN AT THE BARBER SHOP

For weeks you check your
12-year-old profile in car windows,
pinning your 'fro back at the sides,
searching the internet for photos of
"hairstyles for mixed-race boys".
Finally, after a life of home cuts,
you are ready.
On a grimy street, the Barber Shop smells
of sweat/testosterone/spiced aftershave.
I walk tall into that man space and
we wait with the big guys queued up for
twists & fades/ buzz cuts/ flat tops.
I watch you teetering on the edge
of manhood, forcing yourself into the seat,
panicked that I'll chat to the young man
standing keen with clippers.
He knows what he wants, I say,
staying true to our promise
that I won't show you up.
Heaps of curls pile on the Barber Shop floor.
I cannot watch; I'll come back when it's done.
That's fine, Mum, you say, loudly, in earshot,
and then mouth, *Please don't go, Mum*.
On my return, there you sit
fresh-clipped scalp, knife-sharp fade,
small shelled ears not seen since babyhood,
and then you smile and I know you will
slay hearts and the boy has gone
and a man glitters and sparks.
Stunned in pride I whisper,
Job well done.

MIXED-UP

Mum loves her blue-eyed new-born. Nurse notices I have long, tapered fingers. *Perhaps she will play the cello.* Mum notices that I am very pale and perhaps, as mixed-race babies do, I'll darken. I don't darken, nor do I learn to play the cello. My Martinican grandmother sees me and immediately declares that I have *peau sauvée*, saved skin.

It's break-time in secondary school and Harry walks over to me and shouts *Bushchild your mum's a n*****, isn't she?* I slap him hard because even though I don't fully understand the word, I know it carries all the violence of a slavedriver's whip. I must protect her.

I'm 14 and standing on the platform at Kings Cross tube station, visiting London from North Wales. A group of Black girls in shiny coats yell, from across the platform, *Are you black or white or half caste — or what?* I shout *half cast* and walk away, fast, burning with shame because there is no answer which feels right or will make them like me.

We are in Notting Hill, carnival bass thumping, jumping up with my white friends who look around and say *Hey, we are the only white people dancing here.* I feel my blood rise because I am NOT *white people* so don't count me amongst your own.

I am in Kingston, Jamaica on a field trip, walking to the Supermarket for my weekly shop. Men drive past me, turn the car around and crawl slowly alongside. I am *empress, sexy brown skin, brown gal, browning, red skin, yellow gal, white girl.* I am money/island escape. One man wants to *smell my cunt.*

It's bedtime and my son asks *Do you wish you were just a little bit darker so people would know straight away?* No, I love being the way I am, because that's me. *Yeah, whatever, Mum, if you say so, but, if you're not Black, why do you read so many books about Black pain?*

I'm at a conference in the US. I refer to myself as *Mixed Race* but the Professor of African American Literature shouts *You don't call yourself Black, girlfriend, what is wrong with you?* Well, *Mixed,* I explain quickly, is an acceptable term in the UK and some people may be offended if I, blonde-hair-blue-eyes-pale-skin, claim Black for myself.

I am viewing a house in Leeds. Mum is 71 and needs a new home after the divorce. The landlady's face freezes as she opens the door. Mum stands, calm and resplendent in her red velvet coat. To every question Mum asks, the landlady answers me. Cannot, will not look Mum in the eye. I am furious. I wait outside. As we drive home Mum says *I didn't even notice, Emily, I just thought she was a bit rough around the edges.*

I'm 44. You can ask if you can touch my hair. *It feels softer than expected.* Or just dig your hands deep into my 'fro, which you do, on just about every night out, uninvited. Ask me the same old questions. *Where are you from, really.* But you'll never know the story. It's too tangled for you, too knotted, too tragic, too joyous, too dense. You don't have the time. It crosses too many continents. It's too mixed-up.

ORISHA

When she speaks the name of the Orisha,
the one we should not utter,
the tight room shifts, then shrinks.

She doesn't know, they whisper,
what she has brought upon us,
and there is no undoing.

Merciless Yoruba deity, unleashed
into a parlour so quiet
falling mangos echo in the yard,
only hushed sorrys can be made
for being on the outside,
for not knowing the power
of this beckoning.
Ka rele.
Now let us go home.

CROSSROAD BLUES

When I am no longer taut,
when arms sag along with jowls
and my body blurs around its edges,
when nice cups of tea punctuate the day,
will the longing cease?

Will the daily rhythm of a walk
through winter woods, along a clear path,
to note fluctuations of the seasons
stop the stretching of my arms
for things not good or possible?

No, let me stay old blues she-devil
selling her soul for love & music,
my wizened & trembling hands
making my guitar sing & spellbind,
while the yearning cuts deep
through tainted veins, keeping me
fixed to the crossroads

ANANSI'S SILENCE

Anansi, I have a handful of tears. Will you take them?
I have called upon you, my Ghanaian god of antiquity,
let you rope a knotted web around my shoulders,
caress my calves with thick, crabbed legs and yet
you hide your gifts from me. I am un-storied.

I have little else to offer at your altar. Guide
me towards your knowing. Whisper
stories of your cunning, let me see how I can dance
and shift my shape like shadows in the gloaming.
Anansi, tell me. Cure my longing.

Hex me, cast a spell of bone and herb,
let it stench metallic, like lightning striking roofs of zinc.
Let Drybone climb upon my back, wrap his
pincer thighs around my soft rolling hips,
knifing skin with a corpse's nails, becoming ever heavier,
sinking souls with every step.

Dig your spider's teeth into my breastbone.
With your small pink tongue lap
the sweetness of my sweat from deep between thighs.
Thread my poems with tricks and curses,
sew my poet's mouth with vines so I may never speak again.
Just whisper me a tale.

Anansi, I have a mouthful of blood. Will you kiss me?
I hear nothing. I cannot know the path to wisdom and
am bruised from wanting, tendons strung like telegraph wire.
Even if the telling blasts my ears, breaks my back,
bless me with your spool of tales.
Entangle me. Story me.

AURAI

Whirl up, wind,
pull me from daily living,
from sandwiches and summer fetes
from stifled smiles, talk that's small,
to rise and fall in screaming squalls.

Whirl up, wind,
drag me through the thunder clouds,
smash me on the lakeshore rocks,
scatter me on cresting waves
to break the cycle of my days.

Whirl up, wind,
rip the binding seal of hearts,
slam the shell and spill the yoke
so soul's taboos, the silent things,
sing airborne on the swallow's wings.

BLOOD PRESSURE

I drink 6 units a week or maybe 8? At the window,
Spring sunlight fingers NHS blinds.

Nurse looks doubtful. Which is it? Computer
waits patiently for correct numbers.

8. It's 8. *And I eat no meat and run weekly*, but this
does not impress nurse and now it's time for blood pressure.

Gripped by the machine with its own breath a compression
around my upper arm, an ancestor's manacle or

a harassing man in a club holding me away
from the comfort of friends,

while my heart drums faster, I try to remember
the visualisation technique involving the pool

below the waterfall, or was it the deserted beach
the therapist said I should walk on, and when I look back

the sand should swallow visualized footprints, but
my body betrays me, pounding-meteor-pushing

wild blood through tight veins like rush hour. All I can say is
I have white coat syndrome and behind her I see again the

tattered SPOTTING SIGNS OF STROKE poster and
still the numbers rise so I pray she just gives me stronger pills

and unclamps me from this contraption-of-reckoning
into the beckoning Spring,

so I can love it back with all my abnormally
fast-pumping-blood-pressured-heart.

MOON-PULLED

I'm waiting in the cubicle until the coast is clear
to dash out and wash my moon cup,
after pouring away the last few hours
of my warm blood.

At the sink, the drama of white porcelain
against bright redness is searing.
I burn with the need to wash this all clean.

Hands frantic, praying that another
woman doesn't come in and see
all this disgusting mess –
another woman who also bleeds.

So why does all of this stay hidden
from lovers/kids/sisters/mothers as we
squirrel away tampons in drawers,
hoping that they remain our secrets?

Why do we discuss new menstruation knickers
in hushed tones as if we are plotting a revolution,
when we should be plotting a revolution.

For we are moon-pulled, our wombs holy,
connecting us to the ocean tides, earth and stars.
Our 28 days cycles are not by chance,
for the whole universe rests in our blood cycles,

which could be celebrated by lovers
shouting out of open windows
Her period has begun and waving
sanitary towels like carnival flags.

And then I hear the click of the door and rinse out
the last shameful stain and pretend
to be applying my red lipstick.
That's a lovely colour,
she says.

DAVID ATTENBOROUGH AND I

Under a starless sky, David Attenborough and I
are walking in dense forest.
David stops to show me rarest lichens,
alive with light in darkness and flowers
throwing pungent scents into the night.

The thick air hums with noise and I tell David
I'm worried we are lost among these trees,
but David takes my hand and says,
A little lostness can be a good thing.

Then David tells me, with a crinkly smile,
something incredibly profound about
the planet
its fragility
the future of our race,
yet I can only think *my toes are cold*
and wake to find the duvet slipping,
David's words forever lost.

MORNING GRAPES

I don't know why
you bring me grapes
this morning,
their skin taut
in the pale light.
Outside the brightening
window the moon
still lingers,
but I guess it's just to say
that after twenty years
we are still worth
a grape or two,
so let's eat grapes
on this Spring morning,
and if you stain the pillow
I won't
even
mention it.

BLAZE

What is this love with the heat turned down,
fire dying but the ashes still warm?
Should I watch them grow cold,
scrape them up,
store them safe,
keep them close,
and when the time is right
release love's dust into the wind,
a farewell, a funeral?

Or should I gather twigs
and bits of dried moss,
tenderly place them
around glowing embers,
blow gently, steadily
and watch the blaze climb,
the flames lick
until it's fierce enough,
wild enough
to burn down
forests?

DRILLING

So years of fury and
tongue-fire have
formed layers
of sediment, now stone,
over the soft centre of
our hearts.

We've lived our youth,
now middle age, with
the knowledge that we differ
like drought and flood,
our sleep-orbits out of kilter –
when I rise you slumber –
we warm our bed in shifts,
we pelt our words like darts.

But I'm ready to start
drilling through basalt and crust,
past mantle to inner core,
to make new passages
for love's song.

I have my helmet and googles on,
and armed with drill in hand,
I'm going in deep, so when I'm done,
you'll wake up with no idea
why your tongue is honeyed
with sweet words, and your arms
ache to embrace.

LOVE SONG FOR A NEW DAY

Morning, after a night of rearranging limbs in sleep,
so we can better curl our warmth
into each other's bodies,
we wake to argue over who makes coffee.

Before I slip from my side of the bed,
you lightly hold my face and say,
After decades, we still fit, you and I,
like a door in a jamb, a link in a chain
fused on the same axis.
Know that my love for you
is deep, unending,
yet still fresh

Our children descend, locked in a quarrel,
but your words still hang vivid
above the duvet,
drenched in morning light.

III. WATER RITES

I CRIED FOR SMALLER THINGS

Out there on the lake
where the lapwing's glide,
wind slaps water into frenzied waves
while on the fell tops ragged sheep
turn bottoms to the sleet
and wait for warmer days.

Let this squall dry tears
cried for smaller things
than lake and land and sky.

Let it burn my cheek
and hurl me into clashes
between the clouds and moors
to be guided home at dusk
by the curlew's call.

DIVINITY

If no God, what then?
To fight the shadows?
Or has the tree felled
to make the small coffins
that haunt my waking nights
grown a new branch?

Or perhaps a celestial imprint
crafted by a midwife's hand
can be found in the knot of my navel,
or gliding in the pull of river current
teasing the hairs of my arms
as I swim upstream,

or hidden in glossy vegetables
brought home to the dinner table
from Yorkshire earth,

or nestling in the elastic stretch of legs before sleep
or in the silence of the waking moment,
before swarms of heartaches fly in to assault?
Is it here the divine resides?

AND SO, WE FALL

We are light as puffs of dandelion,
long-grass drifting,
as you collect owls' feathers
forget-me-nots
a sheep's jawbone
a heart-shaped stone.

Together, watching the fat bee
penetrate the purple-chasmed foxglove,
we agree they are the perfect fit,
made for each other.

I forget about the illness
nearly claiming you, laugh,
watching butterflies courting.

Lying in the sheep field,
spitting cherry stones,
sunshine-squinting,
we find faces in the old oak's trunk.

Then the farmer passes,
head-down, heavy-booted,
sheepdog snarling,
does not return our smiles,
steeping us in our
not-from-round-here-ness.

And so we fall earth-bound,
weighted, back to burden,
back to life,
surrounded by
airborne summer puffs.

RIVER RITES

I seek baptism
absolution from life's sins,
from fighting loud enough
to scare our neighbours,
from ruptured family,
cancer curse.

So, water-borne, I thrust
my brown body across
the cloud-rippled sky,
Afro-lady cum pond-skater.

With each stroke you tame me, Yorkshire river,
with each stroke you claim me, Yorkshire river,

I, daughter of diasporic waters,
each long muscle flexing,
now unfettered, darting towards
the sun's reflections,
I shed history like a shattered shell.
These are my river rites,
my resurrection complete.

AFTER THE RAIN

We fight
your words cut me down
rain blasts the windows
the doorframe shakes
I roar

I sit on a bench
I wait
watch rain fall rhythmic
on my skin

after the rain
my curls cling tight
droplets caught in webs
fall and wash me clean
like river stones
smooth-edged
no smell of sweat or fight
my body
riverbed calm

I return home
I cannnot remember rage

only rain

RICHES

On the shoreline,
little Rose brings me treasures,
shimmering shells
metallic pebbles bright with glitter
arching seagull feathers to top
patted mounds of sand
minuscule bits of glass
edges smooth-sculpted
by wave and time.
Now, she tells me,
you are rich

SCYTHING

You are scything in the lower field, cotton
shirt sleeves rolled tight, waist-high
in dewy summer grass. The evening light

turns your thinning hair into an amber crown;
the sweep of your arms is clean, your swinging
cut a heartbeat, the blade a breath,

or whispering wind in treetops,
swish of water over stones.
You wish you were a farmer, holding

the scythe of ancestors, rituals of the old ways,
yet your hands are soft from writing,
dirt under fingernails cleaned daily.

The sun throws its last rays into the clouds
and slips behind the ridge. You stop and stretch,
greeting a completeness never gifted by the pen.

DAD'S SOLSTICE

You're laughing, face backlit against the sloping sun,
tapping tent pegs through faded canvas with a flat stone,

just right for the job you say, and I wonder why, every summer,
you bother to take us here to *Llyn yr Adar*, lake of birds,

through foxglove spires, sucking bog, towering bracken
as we complain incessantly – up mountain paths, packs hefty,

shoes rubbing – for who cares that it's the longest day? But you
have found the perfect pitch, built your crackling fire with tiny bits

of grey-dry gorse – though we refused to help – and beans now bubble
in the tin, potatoes foil-wrapped for embers yet-to-come.

Your heart-light mood's unshakable, though we disapprove
your every move. But when the meadow pipits cease their song

and bog myrtle throws its limey scent into the gloaming,
the midsummer moon hangs low over the blackened lake,

and from my sleeping bag I start to understand the yearly ritual, Dad,
your pilgrimage to honour earth's celestial tilt.

THRESHOLD

When you fall towards me, Dad,
the earth tilts.
You are wearing a Santa hat and you hit the tiles hard.
I feel the crack of it. Like metal scraping teeth.

I lift your head onto my lap
screaming for help, screaming Nana,
noticing the strange angle of your legs
in their bottle-green jumbo cords.

I hear the thud of earth on your coffin.

In my panic I am useless,
frozen in your silence.
Only when your eyes open
do I breathe.

Guiding you to the sofa,
I stroke your knees, your hands,
I rub your back.
I want to piece you back together again.

Don't make a fuss, you say,
Just a tea with two sugars and don't call the doc.
Just a slip on the doorway.

I leave you with Nana.
I stand in the doorway that ruptured the day.

It's a hard-to-navigate threshold, Dad.
Far too easy for old adventurers
to slip through.

BOAT ON PEBBLES
For Dad

Today you're in your pants, you mad old man,
heaving your blue rowboat up the pebbled shore,
refusing help and ignoring calls – *Please, put on a t-shirt, Dad!*

That Christmas I thought you'd just had too much cider,
or were drunk on reunion excitement and lots
of sentimental chat around a winter fire,
but Nana acted quick as 999.

On your ward a teenager wakes every night,
pacing up and down and talking, talking,
until Nurse Anne leads him gently back to bed,
while every word you mumble we greet with frantic nods,
every movement a wonder of will,
but when I stroke your hand you tell me that you hate it here,
can't handle this for long, so set me free.

Your best friend breaks you out
with letters to consultants insisting on your liberty,
and for six months you and Nana cope at home,
silent, stoic.

Your balance shattered, parquet floors roll and pitch
like stormy seas; carpets crack with crevasses
whose fault lines swallow the physio's advice.

At night you speak of dizzying dreams,
flotsam spinning from the crests of boiling waves,
and wake hourly to sheets slick with sweat.

Nana helps you find your words
catch your words, share your words;
hurries to your bedside when you holler

for another cuppa, please,
as you try to stop your spidery scrawl
from bursting through the lines of little notebooks;
helps you walk straight and unassisted.

That winter when you come to visit,
you don't let us hold your hand,
when, on quaking legs, you climb the slippery crag,
admire the viewpoint as we hawk your every move,
and you get cross at all the pills and all the fuss.

And now you insist on pulling up your boat –
no help, thanks – and in your pants
because it's hot and thirsty work,
and so goes your stroke with death, Dad,
and you strike on, stubborn as an old blue rowing boat
that won't ground onto shore.

COUSIN REMEMBERED

To cousin Julia, who died of cancer aged 34

I remember your outline
as you lay on the bed beside me,
stilled by the tropical night,
black hair pooling on a moonlit pillow,
long body soft and young –
valley of waist, contour of hip, plateau of thigh.
You were fast to anger, quick to love,
thrumming and pulsing with life.

On a Cevenol mid-summer's day,
heat puddles the air;
I take this bonny son of yours
to your grave in the old walled cemetery,
watch useless as his tears ripple and pool,
falling on the baking earth
which cradles your vanished body.

We gather bunches of lavender
from where you lie.
Across the hot gravestones
he chases a darting lizard,
glistening emerald in the light.
Tears dry as he throws back his head,
laughter rising up
towards the sun.

AFTER YOUR DIAGNOSIS

I set about planting beans, sunflowers
tomatoes, nasturtiums, beetroots
in such a frenzy that I lost track
of which were foxgloves
and which were carrots,
but with each seed
a prayer: may this growing
promise harvests
gathered with
a lighter heart.

BLACKBERRIES

You were sick when we last picked blackberries,
pink cap hiding chemo baldness.
For me it was a moment for forgetting,
for you, a hunt for berries.

The sweetest are the highest,
nestling ripe in coils of thorns,
tempting pickers to skin-pierce
for summer's mouth-flood juices.

You and I, picking side-by-side,
these were all my wishes,
to walk amongst the bramble briars
and plan the sweetest dishes.

IV: FELL

RUNNING LOST

Under low, leaden Cumbrian skies
the endless snake of tarmac takes me
to yet another wind-bitten farm
with squatting cattle sheds.

The sweat grows cold on my body
as I knock on a farmhouse door,
holding my steaming breath.
Above me starlings settle in naked trees
as storm clouds gather and darken
in this green desert without markers,
that will not reveal itself.

"I'm lost, I've been running for miles;
they said keep turning left."
"Aye, keep turning left,"
he tells me, with mocking eyes.
"You're 'bout three miles away."

I'm a woman out of place and foolishly unwise
in this bleak winter landscape,
but my bright orange trainers
now streak brazenly across the cowpats
homeward bound.

WILD CAMP

Three men stop me on my climb.
Are you sure you have enough water?
But where will you be staying the night?
Do you really know where you're going?

On the summit I watch, from my tent,
the gloaming stretch long fingers across the sky.
All is silent; I am perched high
above bird song, the bleat of sheep,
the rumble of the roads.

Soon I am swallowed by night's
her dark trailing cloak, stained with
the glittering swirl of the milky way,
the corpses of a thousand stars.

I shall sleep safely here
halfway between earth and sky,
raised closer to the moon,
away from doubting men and
their questions.

SNOWDON LILY

You are reluctant to leave behind your mountain biking,
your pals, the i-phone, the skate park,
to climb a Welsh mountain with your mum.

As we walk, I tell you about the Snowdon lily,
delicate white alpine, green-veined,
that blooms alone, out of reach, in rock crevices,
found only on these rough slopes. You yawn.

We start the ascent up the Tryfan rockface
and the 13-year-old bravado is soon gone,
the *Mum, watch me do this no-handed*
replaced by careful concentration, part fear, part flow.

We look at the ravine beneath us,
cloud shadows moving like whales across the valley,
the wind carrying the clean scent
of crashing waterfalls of glacial rock.

You are silent now,
your nimble body finding each crevice
to bear yourself up the glacial cleft,
as clouds claim the jagged tops above you.

When we summit, you embrace me,
our knees still adrenaline weak,
and tell me that mountains are not just about climbing –
they are *an experience.* You get it now.

I watch you standing halfway between earth and sky,
soft curls catching weak fingers of sunlight,
and try and commit to memory
every detail of this moment,
rare as a Snowdon lily.

UNFORGETTING

I came here to forget
but the mosses are emerald galaxies,
lichens creep like clouds
on shattered glacial rocks,
blood-red rowan berries
drop into glistening, icy flows
and the rattle of bell heathers
carry whispers of your name.

This valley holds me in its palm
and each of its ridged fingers
point towards the sky,
where your eyes are
reflected in each opening
between the gathering clouds.

WHEN THE MIND STARTS TO ROAM

We run gritty trail and puddled track
in gripping, sticky mud,
past ragged sheep too cold to move,
over turnip-scattered January fields
framed by skeletons of trees.

35km and the mind starts to roam –
a mirage of a Spanish bull
and red-caped toreador, poised to fight,
invades the corner of my eye,
until it grasps the gaps
between the contours
the hollows of encircling arms.

Witness now collapse of distance
between here and any ending,
all time and space in flux and flow,
housed here in leg and foot and earth.

RAWTON POT

We stand small, mud-footed, tight-limbed
on the edge of the gaping fissure,
high on a pockmarked fell
whose watery guts flee light.

It allowed us to climb its back,
peer into its jaws, feel
the fine mist of its catacombed breath
on our red cheeks, hear its waterfalled
belly growl in the pulling darkness.

I long to move closer, finger the luminous ferns
at its throat, stroke the contours of its
stone and water gills, be cradled by its
mossy, star-strewn lungs,
become its disappearing river.

You draw me back from the edge,
for each dream drops differently
into the midnight chasm.
We turn our backs, blessed.
We peered inwards, we left whole.

DUNG BEETLE

Keeper of the fell,
intently progressing
across the mossy path,
tapping out mountain-time
with each spiny leg,
an untrodden carbon puzzle
across my path, not boot-crushed
but complete, in oilslick
incandescent armour,
steady as an ice-age boulder,
patient as a hole-making drip,
flawless as an oak ring, you,
who roll excrement into planets
and mirror each midsummer star
on your shell, show me the universe
in the secrets of your dung.

THE REASON I SLAPPED BARRY

I wasn't sure I meant to mark your face,
wobble your fleshy cheek,
and bring tears to your eyes,
but that grey world of slate
and dripping bracken,
of Croesor and glistening
sheep poo in the drizzle,
was also mine.

Mine, too, the pools of icy water
so clear the bottom looked like
pebbles hung in glass,
so when you dived in after class
your breath was punched
right out of your body.

Mine that ocean-bound valley
flanked by mountains
whose arms reached out
to protect a cwm which
gently flattened towards the sea,
so that every primary school picture
I ever drew was set in mountains
with a cheery sun and thick,
pencil-scribbled clouds.

So when you called me *half caste*
you cast me halfway out of my world,
my homeland, my *mamwlad,*
and that slap was for halving me,
though proving that all of it
was mine in full.

CROSS COUNTRY: WHAT THEY DO IN THE DUNES

My shadow follows me across the empty beach
as I skirt the threshold between sand and ocean;
discount trainers beat a lonely drum
as the noon sun spreads itself across the sky.

My classmates laugh and snog in the white-hot dunes,
and I imagine the press of pink lips,
the feel of teeth-stroking tongue,
untrained searching between thighs.

I dream the taste of handbag-stolen menthols,
illicit drags, cloud-gazing in the marram grass.
So, no sense of victory in my win against class seven,
I ache only for what they do in the dunes.

Y GWYLIAU HAF (THE SUMMER HOLIDAYS)

August drags deep across the Croesor valley,
her cloak tedium-heavy.

Stuck at home, I watch red ants weave over
hot slate, dive into driveway gaps,

and tired ferns retreat in
ruined outhouse nooks.

An abandoned kitten naps
in the coolest oven of the Aga;

a blue-black jackdaw with broken wing
flaps circles in the shed;

the brown hen hides all her eggs,
the black hen finds the fattest worms;

in the lower field, a dead sheep putrefies,
the sweet stink carried on the breeze;

a feasting crow is tethered to the earth
by elastic strings of guts;

maggots, exposed to heat, to light, dance;
the towering bracken starts to brown.

Then, one morning, a promise carried on the chill.
September, and early morning walks to school.

ON LEAVING THE WORLD OF JOHNS

I am the poshest girl in school,
whose hair is too big & bushy,
nose too wide, nostrils like tunnels,
who lives in the sticks,
who wears wellies to school,
whose mum is too black.
French-frog
Sheep-shagger
Stig of the Dump
Bushchild

I am all these things and worse,
says John Wilkinson
who everyday rolls my name around his mouth
then spits it out, scattergun,
on the school bus, raising a rousing chant:
Emily Mar... SHALL Emily Mar... SHALL...
She sounds so posh, that's how she speaks
Emily Mar... SHALL...
My name, remolded, sharpened,
rains down like arrows.

One hunting ground is a teacherless
music lesson. Class join in John's chorus.
I watch my treble and bass clef
fuse in tear-stained ink.

And as I pass in the corridor,
John hits me on the back of the head.
Emily Mar... SHALL!
When he's not flinging my name
he hurls chocolate wrappers, pencils, rubbers.

Night-time is full of dreaming;
I decapitate John, cleanly
with a samurai sword,
only to wake to John
in classrooms, buses, corridors, sports pitches
armed with my name,
hungry for my pain.

Today, I observe that my name Emily
comes from Latin: *Aemilia* meaning *striving, eager,*
as in "I was eager to leave the world of Johns",
or Emily from Greek, meaning *wily* and *persuasive*
as in trickster channelling Anansi's energy,
coaxing with a silver tongue.

John, I note your name, too.
John, meaning *a man who is the customer of a prostitute,*
John, meaning *toilet*
as in: *I'm going to shit on the John,*
on all the Johns,
eagerly.

SWIFT

You need to talk,
so you pack Mum's picnic blanket
and lead me to the waterfall,
a secret place of crashing waters,
your thinking spot,
your sanctuary.

At the water's edge, I watch your dancing hands
backlit by white July sunlight.
You tell me you and Mum,
who *still love each other* and *always will*,
are moving apart, to live in different houses,
better for everyone, a hard decision.

I dive into heart-punching water
then lie on the bank.
I watch you through sun-scrunched eyes
I do not cry. My back feels supple,
my whole body charged with teenage possibility.

You are still trying to explain.
I watch your fingers, your mouth encircle
but never land on the word,
and I think of swifts, who spend six months
airborne, darting, even resting on the wing.
Pilots have found clusters deep in sky-sleep,
drifting cloud-high on twisting thermals.

Mum's blanket throws out scents of mothballs,
bracken, our Welsh farmhouse, slate-cold
in the blaze of summer. This is everything we leave behind.
Your crinkly eyes shine with tears
but I look skywards. Sixteen.
I will live on the wing.

ACKNOWLEDGEMENTS

I am grateful to Tom Brown for his belief in me and for his unending love and kindness. Thank you to my daughter Rose, for listening patiently to my poems and for sharing her own beautiful creations, and to my son Theo for inspiring me – and declaring that poetry was 'dead', thus challenging me to prove him wrong.

Bath of Herbs would not have come together without the mentorship, careful scrutiny and sharp eye of Jacob Ross, who told me I was a poet and encouraged me to share and develop my writing. I am forever grateful, Jacob. Jeremy Poynting has helped edit and shape this work with patience and meticulous precision. Hannah Bannister and Sam Barratt, I am grateful for your work on the cover design and Carol Sorhaindo, I am honoured to have your beautiful painting, 'transformation and renewal', on the front cover. The Peepal Tree Press Readers and Writers group has been a source of support, laughter and inspiration for several years. A special shout out to Khadijah Ibrahiim, Malika Booker, Melanie Abrahams, Sai Murray and Jason Allen-Paisant for helping to create a thriving poetry scene in Leeds. My friends and colleagues at Leeds Beckett University, James McGrath, Nasser Hussain, Rachel Rich and Susan Watkins have encouraged me to bring this book into being. I am grateful.

My Dad, Peter Marshall, has always encouraged me to write. Thank you for your love and faith in me. Liz Ashton-Hill, thank you for being such a wonderful reader of my work and for always responding straight from the heart. Hannah Sherbersky, you know me like a sister and have always helped me grow. Thank you also to my best friends Pascale Gayford and Ruth Thomas, for helping me form the title poem in a budget hostel in Bali. The seeds of the work were sown there, with you both.

Lee Snoding and Bridget Kelly, I am grateful for your friendship and our Friday hikes. With you I can share my love of nature and take on mountains in blizzards and heatwaves. I owe much to my 'Wonder Women' – Katie Brown, Kate Lennie, Yeni Pankhurst and, of course, Rose Farrar. You are sustenance for the soul. Jenny Zobel, my beloved Mum, this collection is dedicated to you. I'm sorry you are not here to see it published, but I still feel your unconditional love, I hear your wisdom and I share your *joie de vivre*. Give thanks.

Thanks to the following for previously published poems:

"A Sweet Mango for Mami", *Smoke*, Issue 67, poetry pamphlet, 2020.
"Dung Beetle", Spelt Magazine, issue 05, 2022.
"The Reason I Slapped Barry", *Stand Magazine*, Vol. 19, No.4. 2022.
"Don't Let the Boy Cut Cane" and "After the Rain", Caribbean Quarterly, Vol 66, Issue 3, 2020.
"Bath of Herbs" and "Cousin Remembered", *The Caribbean Writer*, Vol 34, 2020,
"Fox" and "Running Lost", *Weighted Words*, Peepal Tree Press, 2021.

ABOUT THE AUTHOR

Emily Zobel Marshall is a Reader in Cultural Studies at Leeds Beckett University. Emily's research specialisms are Caribbean literature and Caribbean carnival cultures. She is an expert on the trickster figure in the folklore, oral cultures and literature of the African Diaspora and has published widely in these fields. She has also established a Caribbean Carnival Cultures research platform and network that aims to bring the critical, creative, academic and artistic aspects of carnival into dialogue with one another. She is a regular contributor to BBC radio discussions on racial politics and Caribbean culture. Her books focus on the role of the trickster in Caribbean and African American cultures; her first book, *Anansi's Journey: A Story of Jamaican Cultural Resistance* (2012) was published by the University of the West Indies Press and her second book, *American Trickster: Trauma Tradition and Brer Rabbit*, was published by Rowman and Littlefield in 2019. Emily acknowledges a stimulus to pursuing a literary career to the example of her grandfather, the Martiniquan writer, Joseph Zobel.

She is Vice Chair of the David Oluwale Memorial Association, a charity committed to fighting racism and homelessness, and is a Creative Associate of the art-based youth charity The Geraldine Connor Foundation.